Effortless Happiness

How to Find Your Voice and Finally Ask For What You Really Want

Joyce Buford

Creator of the Uncover Your Hidden Genius Program

Hidden Genius Press

Title: Effortless Happiness - How to Find Your Voice and Finally Ask For What You Really Want

Author: Joyce Buford

Copyright © 2016 by Joyce Buford
All Rights Reserved

Copyeditor: Calvin Black & Jeana DeShazer
Cover Design: Morgan Crane
Interior Design: Calvin Black & Jeana DeShazer

All rights reserved. This book was self-published by the author Joyce Buford under Hidden Genius Press. No part of this book may be reproduced in any form by any means without the express permission of the author. This includes reprints, excerpts, photocopying, recording, or any future means of reproducing text.

If you would like to do any of the above, please seek permission first by contacting us at http://joycebufordempowers.com

Published in the United States by Hidden Genius Press
ISBN: 9780997887402

Dedicated to my ...

Mother – Vona Spencer Tindle who taught me the quality of resilience. She led by example, facing her doubts and fears with action. No matter what struggle she faced, she always took action to overcome. She taught me to put faith in tomorrow, as if tomorrow is a sure thing. Even at the age of 99 years, she still sees herself as a "young doer". I love her zest for life.

Children – who are still teaching me love, patience, and forgiveness. With you by my side, I have faced my darkest challenges, only to find there is indeed peace and happiness on the other side. No challenge is too great and no pain is too deep to dispel.

Thank you for being part of the journey!!

Dogs - Princess and MooMoo – who taught me unconditional love!!

Other Teachers – you are friends, family members, coaches, teachers, lovers, and simply fellow searchers. Each has taught me a thought, an understanding, a principle I would need along this journey.

Thank you for being part of the team that guided me to this life of fulfillment and joy.

- About the Author -

Joyce Buford is a SecondWind Coach, Speaker, Author, and weekly Internet radio host of *SecondWind with Joyce*. As a woman who has experienced transition in her own life, her program focuses on helping clients who have experienced their own transitions, such as divorce, death of a loved one, career change or empty nest syndrome.

She was personally mentored by Jack Canfield, author of the "Chicken Soup for the Soul" book series

Through her unique program and coaching style, Joyce supports clients during their transition to reclaim their true purpose and strengths.

Through her community involvement, entrepreneurship and philanthropy, Joyce has contributed for 30 years.

Joyce is the proud mother of Chris and Lauren. She loves music, travel, and learning. She lives her life on purpose, using and enjoying her talents to get her message out………..living with effortless happiness.

- Contents -

Introduction	1
Uncover Your Hidden Genius	5
7 Types of Individuals	13
What Are Core Values and Why Should I Care About Finding Mine?	19
When Should I Identify Core Values?	23
7 Areas of Life that Must Align with Your Values	29
Why Are Core Values So Important To Living with Effortless Happiness?	33
4 Simple Steps to Identifying Your Core Values	39
Finding Your Top 5 Values	47
Your Top 5 Core Values	54
Living in Your Top 5 Core Values	59

Aligning of Your Core Values With The
Expression Of Your Voice ... 73

7 Areas of Your Life that Contribute
to Your Sense of Effortless Happiness ... 73

   1. Health & Fitness ... 75
   2. Spiritual Fulfillment ... 87
   3. Societal Contribution ... 99
   4. Personal Growth ... 111
   5. Financial Success ... 123
   6. Professional/Career ... 135
   7. Personal Relationships ... 147

Being Conscious of My Values ... 161

Conclusion ... 167

SecondWind Podcasts ... 175

Happiness is your nature. It is not wrong to desire it. What is wrong is seeking it outside when it is inside.

- Ramana Maharshi

Introduction

$$\text{Authentic Self} + \text{Core Values} = \text{Effortless Happiness}$$

You are about to embark on an amazing process of exploration and discovery. I am so glad that you have decided to join me in thinking about and identifying your core values.

I like to think about this process as uncovering hidden treasure. Imagine that you are an archaeologist picking through ancient mounds of dirt and sweeping away dust that has settled through years of time. In order to find your treasure, you need to set up a grid and methodically examine your site section by section, square foot by square foot. Only by taking your time, having a bit of patience, and looking carefully at each square can you determine where the treasure lies.

In this workbook I will lead you through a process of examining your core values. Before we start, I want to encourage you to take your time. Find a place where you aren't distracted, clear a space on your calendar, and commit to going through this process with as few interruptions as possible.

It will take some time, so have patience. The process is repetitive and you may be frustrated in completing the same task over and over. It is important to stick with it to the end. Remember, if you were an archaeologist and left the last sections of your site unexamined you may miss the treasure.

Finally, whatever difficult circumstances you have faced in the past, this process can help lead you to better days. Know that this process of living according to your core values can launch you into an amazing future of happiness and fulfillment.

That is my hope for you. You Can Do It!!!

Unless your heart, your soul, and your whole being are behind every decision you make, the words from your mouth will be empty, and each action will be meaningless. Truth and confidence are the roots of happiness.

- Kathleen Pederse

Uncover Your Hidden Genius

Joyce introduces 6 Easy Steps to Finding Your Genius!

If you've ever wanted to be truly happy with the life you are living, then you're reading the right book. We are going to start by looking at my easy 6-step method for uncovering your hidden genius.

And the good news is that this method works no matter what stage of life you are in.

Step 1: Getting Clear On You

Many people who are new to becoming conscious creators of their lives don't even realize that they need to do this step before they can start the journey. And that's why a lot of people who are trying to reinvent themselves end up failing or circling around and wind up right back where they started – they're missing this critical step.

You'll find that this part of the process goes much more smoothly if you apply these tips and tricks:

Identify your top 5 Core Values. If you don't know your core values, and most don't, please refer to page 40 to easily define them.

Re-evaluate your dreams with your top 5 Core Values to see what would really make you happy.

Once you've gotten clear on who you are and what will make you the happiest, then you can move on to the next step.

Post your top 5 Core Values somewhere you can see them so that anytime you are looking to make a decision you can find it.

Step 2: Engage In Your Purpose

The next thing you need to do is Engage In Your Purpose.

When I first started looking to define my purpose, I made the topic quite heavy. I felt like it was something that was outside of me that I had to go find. When I discovered it was a combination of my talents AND my passions, it made identifying my purpose super simple and a lot more fun!

In order to help you speed this process up for yourself, let me steer you away from these 4 mistakes people make when trying to define their purpose.

Mistake #1: Looking outside of yourself to define what your purpose is.

Mistake #2: Not trusting that the things you are naturally talented at and passionate about.

Mistake #3: Thinking that what you are really good at and is so easy for you is not your answer.

Mistake #4: The belief that you need to work hard to be successful and can't just relax into the possibility of it being easy and fun!

After working with a client to engage in their purpose, we often take a look at whether a meditation or other spiritual practice can assist the client in learning how to tap into their own knowing of what is right for them.

Step 3: Navigate Your Fears & Doubts

At this point you're likely to notice lots of fear and doubt cluttering your mind, learn to manage and eliminate that noise. Replacing the negative thoughts with positive thoughts will help you move fast to claim your happiness.

I've written a few blogs that talk about how I have overcome my fears and doubts throughout my life.

- Are You Making These 3 Mistakes
- How I Got Rid of My Fear And Made A Lifelong Dream Come True
- 6 Steps to Take Your Power Back

You can read them all at:
http://JoyceBufordEmpowers.com

Step 4: Implement Your Plan

After you get those fears and doubts under control it's time to make a plan of action toward living the life you dream about is your next step. For each individual this can look completely different but breaking down the dream into actionable steps with dates for completion and choosing someone to hold you accountable will help you move closer to your dream with ease.

This is the part I love the most! Working with clients to design their plan is where you can be really creative about how you are going to achieve your dream. It's where I can help shine the light on the parts of my clients' soul they have covered up throughout life. Those moments of clarity and confidence are my favorite.

Claiming your areas where you shine is exciting!

Step 5: Uniqueness Is Your Key

Did you know it's a good thing to be unique?

Did you ever get told as a kid to be "seen and not heard" or to "not stand out"?

What if who you were being in those moments was exactly who you needed to be to tap into a life of joy and happiness.

A safe space is created to allow the client to share all of the parts of themselves they've kept hidden. Work on healing those wounds as well as work to foster the qualities that make them unique.

Step 6: Stay Connected

During this step you need to focus on creating a community around you that supports being authentic. This community can include:

- Coaches
- Mentors
- Groups that support your interest (kayaking club or the travel club)
- Friends (old and new)
- Accountability Partners

Working through these 6 steps can take as little as 90 days but for most people it's a yearlong journey. And this journey needs to be repeated every time you are at a stage of reinventing yourself.

The easiest way to make these transition times easier is to have a stable community of support. I'd love to have you find a home here with me and my community. I'd love to help you Uncover Your Hidden Genius and start living a life of happiness!

http://joycebufordempowers.com/uncover-your-hidden-genius

People always ask me, 'You have so much confidence. Where did that come from?' It came from me. One day I decided that I was beautiful, and so I carried out my life as if I was a beautiful girl... it doesn't have anything to do with how the world perceives you.

What matters is what you see.

- Gabourey Sidib

7 Types of Individuals Who Need to Know Their Core Values

1. **Women Entrepreneurs Who Are Looking for More Fulfillment** – Some women create businesses based on a passion but as the business grows they are often faced with the overwhelming challenge of deciding how they want it to grow. There are truly as many options as there are women. Understanding your core values allows you to build the business based on what will make you happy.

   A common obstacle for every woman is reconnecting with her silenced authentic voice. It is that inner voice that has been quieted over time by family, teachers, and self-talk.

2. **Anyone Going Through A Major Life Transition** When life throws you a curve ball, like a death of a loved one, loss of a job, or divorce, you are often forced into a process of reevaluating and reinventing yourself. This process can transform your sense of purpose, your view of the world, and the areas where

you will focus your time. Understanding your core values can help you engage in this process and find your happiness and balance faster.

3. **Managers Who Are Interested In Becoming Better Leaders** – In order to effectively lead, a manager needs to understand her own core values as well as those who work on her team. When hiring new team members, it is especially important to know what their core values are so transition is completed with ease.

4. **Couples Who Are Looking to Communicate Better With One Another** – Often, couples think that they must have the same interests but a diversity of interests can add excitement and opportunities for growth. Understanding each other's core values can help deepen the relationship and provide a framework for navigating difficult conversations.

5. **Women Who Manage Volunteer Teams** – Pulling together a successful team of volunteers means collecting an assortment of highly talented individuals, each with their own unique personalities. As a leader of this diverse group, understanding each individual contributor's core values allows

for the creation of harmony and accelerated success.

6. **Non-Profit Employees** – Committing to work or volunteer for a non-profit organization can be very fulfilling. Some commit to a cause because they believe in its mission.

   Understanding your core values allows you to find ways to reap the benefits of your work and support the mission of the non-profit.

7. **Young Adults** – With so many opportunities available to today's youth, both online and offline, starting the journey of figuring out "what you want to be when you grow up" is expedited by knowing your core values. High school students can use this process to decide which college to attend and what career to pursue. By clarifying their values, college students may decide what major to pick. And, most importantly, young adults can determine to live their life based on their own values and desires instead of choosing what someone else told them they should do.

Love is the master key that opens the gate of happiness.

- Oliver Wendell Holmes

What Are Core Values & Why Should I Care About Finding Mine?

Often you find yourself struggling with life. Your decisions are difficult and you can make the wrong choice. You find yourself out of balance, not reaching your expectations, and failing. The key here is to learn what your authentic self looks like. When you honor your core values you'll find the magic that allows you to live a more authentic and rewarding life.

An example of this concept: You resonate with the word *freedom*, but you work in a job that requires a rigid work schedule. Or perhaps one of your core values is *family*. Your rigid work schedule would conflict with this value as well.

Your job requires that you travel or work, when you really want to spend more time with your family and be more available to them. For a time, this conflict is manageable, but you will become frustrated if you have to maintain it for extended periods.

It all comes down to this: "What do you value the most in your life?".

Do you wake up each morning loving the day and its activities? Are you where you are supposed to be and have a contentment that everything is working as it should?

So, where do Core values come from? Your core values come from the many places and people that you have been exposed to in your life. They can come from family, friends, teachers, and other important people you meet along your path. Values are influenced by where you live, city or rural, and certainly by experiences. We adopt these beliefs and make them part of our authentic self.

As we grow in later years, they can be altered to some extent, but usually not to any great degree of change.

When you hear or read the values that are most meaningful to you, you will resonate with the word. You will have a feeling of comfort, internal knowing, and a deep sense of peace. This is how you can choose a value of importance to you.

Then you can start to make changes in your life that will align with these values and create a life of greater purpose and happiness.

Happiness always looks small while you hold it in your hands, but let it go, and you learn at once how big and precious it is.

-Maxim Gork

When Should I Identify My Core Values?

Based on my own experience in leading workshops, retreats, and in coaching clients privately, you should revisit the following Core Value Exercises every year. This process can help you focus as you plan out what you want to accomplish that year. It's especially important to spend time re-evaluating your core values when you *haven't* accomplished a goal and are feeling a bit of shame or guilt about it.

Additionally, these Core Value Exercises should be revisited when a major life transition occurs like a marriage or divorce, the birth of a child, the death of a loved one, retirement from a job, moving to a different city or country, or the care of a loved one.

People spend a lifetime searching for happiness; looking for peace. They chase idle dreams, addictions, religions, even other people, hoping to fill the emptiness that plagues them. The irony is the only place they ever needed to search with within.

-Ramona L. Anderson

* Maria *

"Working with Joyce to figure out my core values has helped me develop that "go-getter" mentality. It allows me to follow through when I tell my clients I am going to do something which helps me meet my core value of integrity. I take pride in the service I deliver...by knowing that my clients are satisfied."

7 Areas of Life that Must Align with Your Values

Living a happy and peaceful life requires purposeful alignment with your core values.

I have identified 7 areas of your lives which when aligned with your core values will allow you to live a life of effortless happiness

The 7 areas are as follows:

1. **Health & Fitness**
2. **Spiritual Fulfillment**
3. **Societal Contribution**
4. **Personal Growth**
5. **Financial Success**
6. **Professional/Career**
7. **Personal Relationships**

True fulfillment comes from having your core values in alignment with all 7 areas.

If your core value is to be healthy, creating goals in alignment with health will result in success. For Example: the first goal is to improve your health by losing 10 pounds by the end of 3 months. Ways to accomplish this goal will require a strategic plan such as follows: eating more fruits and vegetables daily, implementing an exercise plan, and no drinking of alcohol for 3 months.

However, most individuals I work with find that having your core values aligned in a few areas (3-4) can massively transform their overall feelings of happiness and peace.

Feeling happiness and peace is proof that you are living a life without limits. You are listening to your inner guide and aligning your values to the most significant areas of your life. This will bring you fulfillment, happiness, and peace; that is a life without limits!

Happiness cannot be traveled to, owned, earned, worn or consumed. Happiness is the spiritual experience of living every moment with love, grace, and gratitude.

–Denis Waitley

Why Are Core Values So Important To Living with Effortless Happiness?

If you are working and living in your core values, then happiness becomes effortless.

For every single person I have ever met, the only thing standing in the way between them and happiness is choice.

The choice to be happy versus the choice to succumb to doubts and fears, or people's demands and suggestions.

When you choose to be happy, you also choose to push through whatever doubts and fears you might have.

This is a moment to moment choice.

While your doubts and fears never truly go away, as you collect more and more tools to deal with these thoughts you can start looking at these fears and doubts as stepping stones in your own growth.

On a deeper level you are already complete. When you realize that, there is a playful, joyous energy behind what you do.

- Eckhart Tolle

✱ Michelle ✱

"It made me realize that I had everything flip-flopped: that I was living and working and doing and chasing the business at the sacrifice of my core values which had more to do with family and relationships and fun and happiness. Once I realized what I was doing and made that shift everything felt just right.

It is inevitable. Everything will fall into place if you're living in the spot where you're aligned with your core values. How could you put a price on that?"

4 Simple Steps to Identifying YOUR Core Values

Step 1:

Take 5 Minutes to Review the List of Core Values.

On the following 3 pages, you will select words to identify your values. Some are very similar in meaning, try not to duplicate similar words. Choose the words that best describe your values.

Acceptance	Country
Accessibility	Creativity
Accomplishment	Devotion
Accountability	Discovery
Adventure	Diversity
Approval	Education
Artistry	Emotional Health
Authenticity	Empathy
Beauty	Feeling Energized
Being Extraordinary	Enlightenment
Being of Service	Environment
Brevity	Excellence
Building	Expression
Career	Fairness
Caring	Faith
Challenges	Fame
Chastity	Family
Children	Fidelity
Clarity	Fitness
Commitment	Flexibility
Communication	Focus
Community	Freedom
Compassion	Friendship
Competition	Generosity
Conformity	Goal Achieving
Connection	God
Consciousness	Goddess
Consistency	Good Design
Contribution	Governance

Grace	Looking Good
Gratitude	Love
Greatness	Loyalty
Growth	Making a Difference
Having Fun	Marriage
Healing	Mastery
Health	Meditation
Holidays	Mind Development
Holiness	Ministry
Home	Mission
Honesty	Money
Humility	Morality
Humor	Myself
Imagination	No-Judgment
Improvement	Nurturing
Influence	Open-mindedness
Inspiration	Organization
Integrity	Originality
Intelligence	Parenting
Intention	Participation
Interdependence	Passion
Intimacy	Peace
Justice	Persistence
Kindness	Picty
Laughter	Play
Leadership	Playfulness
Learning	Pleasure
Listening	Power
Longevity	Productivity

Propriety
Providing
Purpose
Radiance
Recognition
Relationships
Relaxation
Religion
Respect
Responsibility
Self-expression
Self-realization
Sense of Humor
Service
Sharing
Sobriety
Spirituality
Spreading light
Strength

Success
Support
Teaching
The Future
Travel
Trust
Truth
Understanding
Unity
Variety
Wealth
Willingness
Winning
Work

Step 2:

Go through the list of Core Values and circle the top 10 words that you identify most with.

Be sure to select the 10 words that are the best description of 'what matters most' to you.

Hint: Some people report feeling 'lighter' when they read a certain word that wants to be a part of their life.

Step 3:

Please write the 10 circled words below in any order.

1. _____

2. _____

3. _____

4. _____

5. _____

6. _____

7. _____

8. _____

9. _____

10. _____

Group all similar values together from the list of values you just transferred to this sheet. If any of them have similar meanings to you, omit all but one and add another word from the Core Values Master list.

Example: Honesty and Integrity may mean the same thing to you. You don't want to have similar meaning words. Ideally, we are looking for 5-10 different core values that you hold dear.

Step 4:

Go through these Steps of Value Clarification in order to identify your Primary Core Value.

> WARNING! Don't cheat on this next part! Go through this exercise exactly as I instruct so that you can be absolutely clear on your core values.

Finding Your Top 5 Core Values

Now Let's Refine Your Top 10 List to 5!

On the next 5 pages you will now Compare Your Top 10 Words from page 44 to Find Your #1 Core Value. Carry the winning value down to begin each new comparison.

Top 10 Core Values Example:

1. Love
2. Travel
3. Beauty
4. Community
5. Freedom
6. Growth
7. Family
8. Spirituality
9. Money
10. Productive

Comparison Example:

(1) Love	vs.	(2) Travel	=	(2) Travel
(2) Travel	vs.	(3) Beauty	=	(2) Travel
(3) Travel	vs.	(4) Community	=	(4) Community
(4) Community	vs.	(5) Freedom	=	(5) Freedom
(5) Freedom	vs.	(6) Growth	=	(5) Freedom
(6) Freedom	vs.	(7) Family	=	(7) Family
(7) Family	vs.	(8) Spirituality	=	(7) Family
(8) Family	vs.	(9) Money	=	(7) Family
(7) Family	vs.	(10) Productive	=	(7) Family

CORE VALUE #1 = Family

Drop "Family" from the comparison rotation as it has moved to My Top Core Value List on page 54. Repeat the comparison exercise without Family.

Note: If you have trouble with this exercise? Check out this video:

http://JoyceBufordEmpowers.com/Core-Values-Elimination-Exercise

Core Values Elimination Exercise Round #1

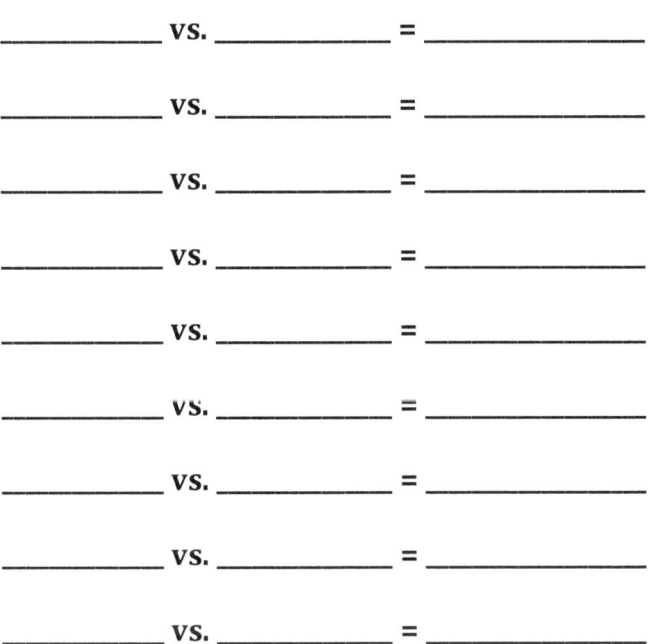

Write the Winner of Round 1 Here and on Page 54

CORE VALUE #1:

_____

Core Values Elimination Exercise Round #2

Please remove Core Value #1 from this round of comparisons. Remember to carry the winning value on each line to begin each new comparison. Compare the remaining 9 core values to find your #2 value.

_____ vs. _____ = _____

_____ vs. _____ = _____

_____ vs. _____ = _____

_____ vs. _____ = _____

_____ vs. _____ = _____

_____ vs. _____ = _____

_____ vs. _____ = _____

_____ vs. _____ = _____

Write the Winner of Round 2 Here and on Page 54

CORE VALUE #2:

_____

Core Values Elimination Exercise Round #3

Please remove Core Values #1 and #2 from this round of comparisons. You should now have 8 remaining core values. Remember to carry the winning value on each line to begin each new comparison. Compare the remaining 8 core values to find your #3 value.

_____ vs. _____ = _____

_____ vs. _____ = _____

_____ vs. _____ = _____

_____ vs. _____ = _____

_____ vs. _____ = _____

_____ vs. _____ = _____

_____ vs. _____ = _____

Write the Winner of Round 3 Here and on Page 54

CORE VALUE #3:

_____

Core Values Elimination Exercise Round #4

You should now have 7 remaining core values. Eliminate the core values you have already identified. Remember to carry the winning value on each line to begin each new comparison. Compare the remaining 7 core values to find your #4 value.

_____ vs. _____ = _____

_____ vs. _____ = _____

_____ vs. _____ = _____

_____ vs. _____ = _____

_____ vs. _____ = _____

_____ vs. _____ = _____

Write the Winner of Round 4 Here and on Page 54

CORE VALUE #4:

_____

Core Values Elimination Exercise Round #5

You should now have 6 remaining core values. Eliminate the core values you have already identified. Remember to carry the winning value on each line to begin each new comparison. Compare the remaining 6 core values to find your #5 value.

_____ vs. _____ = _____

_____ vs. _____ = _____

_____ vs. _____ = _____

_____ vs. _____ = _____

_____ vs. _____ = _____

Write the Winner of Round 5 Here and on Page 54

CORE VALUE #5:

_____

My Top 5 Core Values

You should now have 5 core values listed below. These are your Top 5 Core Values.

#1 _____

#2 _____

#3 _____

#4 _____

#5 _____

*Happiness is not a state to arrive at,
but a manner of traveling.*

– Margaret Lee Runbeck

❋ Heather ❋

"There's so much that I feel is important and being able to settle down to those core values helps me focus. Even my daughter has noticed a difference in how I relate to my clients now. Doing the core values helps me show up and be present in my life and my work."

Living In Your Top 5 Core Values

Now let's talk about how you are currently living or not living according to your core values.

For each of the 5 core values I'm asking you to evaluate how you relate to this value in 3 ways.

Being aware of the importance of each value in adding quality, depth, peace and joy to your life is worth taking your time on this exercise.

Core Value #1: _____

Describe how you relate to the word. This may not be how Webster describes it, but how you understand and use this value in your life:

Evaluate how are you presently living your life with this value:

How can you incorporate the use of this value more in your life:

Core Value #2: _____

Describe how you relate to the word. This may not be how Webster describes it, but how you understand and use this value in your life:

Evaluate how are you presently living your life with this value:

How can you incorporate the use of this value more in your life:

Core Value #3: _____

Describe how you relate to the word. This may not be how Webster describes it, but how you understand and use this value in your life:

Evaluate how are you presently living your life with this value:

How can you incorporate the use of this value more in your life:

Core Value #4: _____

Describe how you relate to the word. This may not be how Webster describes it, but how you understand and use this value in your life:

Evaluate how are you presently living your life with this value:

How can you incorporate the use of this value more in your life:

Core Value #5: _____

Describe how you relate to the word. This may not be how Webster describes it, but how you understand and use this value in your life:

Evaluate how are you presently living your life with this value:

How can you incorporate the use of this value more in your life:

Happiness depends upon ourselves.

– Aristotle

Aligning of Your Core Values With The Expression Of Your Voice

Now that you know your core values it's time to start expressing what you truly desire with each decision you are faced to make.

Yes I know that's going to be a lot of decisions but I promise that over time it'll get easier and easier.

In working with my private coaching clients, I have found that if you focused on what your core values are, you can more easily express what is true for you in each and every situation.

I find it helpful to apply my core values to 7 distinct areas of my life to fully experience effortless happiness. There is no such thing as a perfect alignment it is more of a balance each and every moment of the day.

7 Areas of Your Life that Contribute to Your Sense of Effortless Happiness

1. Health & Fitness
2. Spiritual Fulfillment
3. Societal Contribution

4. **Personal Growth**
5. **Financial Success**
6. **Professional/Career**
7. **Personal Relationships**

During the next section of the book you are going to walk through a few exercises that will help you align your core values with your daily activities. Thus, you learn how to ask for what you want in each and every situation you face.

Ultimately, my hope is that if you know what you want and are able to ask for it – you'll find yourself living a life of Effortless Happiness!

Reflections on what it would take for Me to experience Effortless Happiness when it comes to my...

Health & Fitness Desires

What would effortless happiness look like as it relates to my Health & Fitness Desires?

Core Value #1

Not being in alignment with _____(Insert Core Value #1) as it relates to my Health & Fitness Desires looks like...

Being in alignment with _____ (Insert Core Value #1) as it relates to my Health & Fitness Desires looks like…

What are 3 requests I can make of myself and others to support me in expressing my voice as it relates to my Health & Fitness desires.

1.

2.

3.

What fears & doubts come up in regards to asking for what you want in these situations?

Core Value #2

Not being in alignment with _____(Insert Core Value #2) as it relates to my Health & Fitness Desires looks like…

Being in alignment with _____ (Insert Core Value #2) as it relates to my Health & Fitness Desires looks like…

What are 3 requests I can make of myself and others to support me in expressing my voice as it relates to my Health & Fitness desires.

1.

2.

3.

What fears & doubts come up in regards to asking for what you want in these situations?

Core Value #3

Not being in alignment with _____(Insert Core Value #3) as it relates to my Health & Fitness Desires looks like…

Being in alignment with _____ (Insert Core Value #3) as it relates to my Health & Fitness Desires looks like…

What are 3 requests I can make of myself and others to support me in expressing my voice as it relates to my Health & Fitness desires.

1.

2.

3.

What fears & doubts come up in regards to asking for what you want in these situations?

Core Value #4

Not being in alignment with _____(Insert Core Value #4) as it relates to my Health & Fitness Desires looks like…

Being in alignment with _____ (Insert Core Value #4) as it relates to my Health & Fitness Desires looks like…

What are 3 requests I can make of myself and others to support me in expressing my voice as it relates to my Health & Fitness desires.

1.

2.

3.

What fears & doubts come up in regards to asking for what you want in these situations?

Core Value #5

Not being in alignment with _____ (Insert Core Value #5) as it relates to my Health & Fitness Desires looks like…

Being in alignment with _____ (Insert Core Value #5) as it relates to my Health & Fitness Desires looks like…

What are 3 requests I can make of myself and others to support me in expressing my voice as it relates to my Health & Fitness desires.

1.

2.

3.

What fears & doubts come up in regards to asking for what you want in these situations?

Reflections on what it would take for Me to experience Effortless Happiness when it comes to my…

Spiritual Fulfillment Desires

What would effortless happiness look like as it relates to my Spiritual Fulfillment Desires?

Core Value #1

Not being in alignment with _____(Insert Core Value #1) as it relates to my Spiritual Fulfillment Desires looks like…

Being in alignment with _____ (Insert Core Value #1) as it relates to my Spiritual Fulfillment Desires looks like…

What are 3 requests I can make of myself and others to support me in expressing my voice as it relates to my Spiritual Fulfillment desires.

1.

2.

3.

What fears & doubts come up in regards to asking for what you want in these situations?

Core Value #2

Not being in alignment with _____(Insert Core Value #2) as it relates to my Spiritual Fulfillment Desires looks like…

Being in alignment with _____ (Insert Core Value #2) as it relates to my Spiritual Fulfillment Desires looks like…

What are 3 requests I can make of myself and others to support me in expressing my voice as it relates to my Spiritual Fulfillment desires.

1.

2.

3.

What fears & doubts come up in regards to asking for what you want in these situations?

Core Value #3

Not being in alignment with _____ (Insert Core Value #3) as it relates to my Spiritual Fulfillment Desires looks like…

Being in alignment with _____ (Insert Core Value #3) as it relates to my Spiritual Fulfillment Desires looks like…

What are 3 requests I can make of myself and others to support me in expressing my voice as it relates to my Spiritual Fulfillment desires.

1.

2.

3.

What fears & doubts come up in regards to asking for what you want in these situations?

Core Value #4

Not being in alignment with _____(Insert Core Value #4) as it relates to my Spiritual Fulfillment Desires looks like…

Being in alignment with _____(Insert Core Value #4) as it relates to my Spiritual Fulfillment Desires looks like…

What are 3 requests I can make of myself and others to support me in expressing my voice as it relates to my Spiritual Fulfillment desires.

1.

2.

3.

What fears & doubts come up in regards to asking for what you want in these situations?

Core Value #5

Not being in alignment with _____ (Insert Core Value #5) as it relates to my Spiritual Fulfillment Desires looks like…

Being in alignment with _____ (Insert Core Value #5) as it relates to my Spiritual Fulfillment Desires looks like…

What are 3 requests I can make of myself and others to support me in expressing my voice as it relates to my Spiritual Fulfillment desires.

1.

2.

3.

What fears & doubts come up in regards to asking for what you want in these situations?

Reflections on what it would take for Me to experience Effortless Happiness when it comes to my…

Societal Contribution Desires

What would effortless happiness look like as it relates to my Societal Contribution Desires?

Core Value #1

Not being in alignment with _____ (Insert Core Value #1) as it relates to my Societal Contribution Desires looks like…

Being in alignment with _____ (Insert Core Value #1) as it relates to my Societal Contribution Desires looks like…

What are 3 requests I can make of myself and others to support me in expressing my voice as it relates to my Societal Contribution desires.

1.

2.

3.

What fears & doubts come up in regards to asking for what you want in these situations?

Core Value #2

Not being in alignment with _____(Insert Core Value #2) as it relates to my Societal Contribution Desires looks like…

Being in alignment with _____ (Insert Core Value #2) as it relates to my Societal Contribution Desires looks like…

What are 3 requests I can make of myself and others to support me in expressing my voice as it relates to my Societal Contribution desires.

1.

2.

3.

What fears & doubts come up in regards to asking for what you want in these situations?

Core Value #3

Not being in alignment with _____(Insert Core Value #3) as it relates to my Societal Contribution Desires looks like…

Being in alignment with _____(Insert Core Value #3) as it relates to my Societal Contribution Desires looks like…

What are 3 requests I can make of myself and others to support me in expressing my voice as it relates to my Societal Contribution desires.

1.

2.

3.

What fears & doubts come up in regards to asking for what you want in these situations?

Core Value #4

Not being in alignment with _____(Insert Core Value #4) as it relates to my Societal Contribution Desires looks like…

Being in alignment with _____ (Insert Core Value #4) as it relates to my Societal Contribution Desires looks like…

What are 3 requests I can make of myself and others to support me in expressing my voice as it relates to my Societal Contribution desires.

1.

2.

3.

What fears & doubts come up in regards to asking for what you want in these situations?

Core Value #5

Not being in alignment with _____(Insert Core Value #5) as it relates to my Societal Contribution Desires looks like...

Being in alignment with _____(Insert Core Value #5) as it relates to my Societal Contribution Desires looks like…

What are 3 requests I can make of myself and others to support me in expressing my voice as it relates to my Societal Contribution desires.

1.

2.

3.

What fears & doubts come up in regards to asking for what you want in these situations?

Reflections on what it would take for Me to experience Effortless Happiness when it comes to my...

Personal Growth Desires

What would effortless happiness look like as it relates to my Personal Growth Desires?

Core Value #1

Not being in alignment with _____(Insert Core Value #1) as it relates to my Personal Growth Desires looks like...

Being in alignment with _____ (Insert Core Value #1) as it relates to my Personal Growth Desires looks like…

What are 3 requests I can make of myself and others to support me in expressing my voice as it relates to my Personal Growth desires.

1.

2.

3.

What fears & doubts come up in regards to asking for what you want in these situations?

Core Value #2

Not being in alignment with _____(Insert Core Value #2) as it relates to my Personal Growth Desires looks like…

Being in alignment with _____ (Insert Core Value #2) as it relates to my Personal Growth Desires looks like…

What are 3 requests I can make of myself and others to support me in expressing my voice as it relates to my Personal Growth desires.

1.

2.

3.

What fears & doubts come up in regards to asking for what you want in these situations?

Core Value #3

Not being in alignment with _____(Insert Core Value #3) as it relates to my Personal Growth Desires looks like…

Being in alignment with _____ (Insert Core Value #3) as it relates to my Personal Growth Desires looks like…

What are 3 requests I can make of myself and others to support me in expressing my voice as it relates to my Personal Growth desires.

1.

2.

3.

What fears & doubts come up in regards to asking for what you want in these situations?

Core Value #4

Not being in alignment with _____(Insert Core Value #4) as it relates to my Personal Growth Desires looks like…

Being in alignment with _____(Insert Core Value #4) as it relates to my Personal Growth Desires looks like…

What are 3 requests I can make of myself and others to support me in expressing my voice as it relates to my Personal Growth desires.

1.

2.

3.

What fears & doubts come up in regards to asking for what you want in these situations?

Core Value #5

Not being in alignment with _____(Insert Core Value #5) as it relates to my Personal Growth Desires looks like…

Being in alignment with _____ (Insert Core Value #5) as it relates to my Personal Growth Desires looks like…

What are 3 requests I can make of myself and others to support me in expressing my voice as it relates to my Personal Growth desires.

1.

2.

3.

What fears & doubts come up in regards to asking for what you want in these situations?

Reflections on what it would take for Me to experience Effortless Happiness when it comes to my...

Financial Success Desires

What would effortless happiness look like as it relates to my Financial Success Desires?

Core Value #1

Not being in alignment with _____(Insert Core Value #1) as it relates to my Financial Success Desires looks like...

Being in alignment with _____ (Insert Core Value #1) as it relates to my Financial Success Desires looks like…

What are 3 requests I can make of myself and others to support me in expressing my voice as it relates to my Financial Success desires.

1.

2.

3.

What fears & doubts come up in regards to asking for what you want in these situations?

Core Value #2

Not being in alignment with _____(Insert Core Value #2) as it relates to my Financial Success Desires looks like…

Being in alignment with _____ (Insert Core Value #2) as it relates to my Financial Success Desires looks like…

What are 3 requests I can make of myself and others to support me in expressing my voice as it relates to my Financial Success desires.

1.

2.

3.

What fears & doubts come up in regards to asking for what you want in these situations?

Core Value #3

Not being in alignment with _____ (Insert Core Value #3) as it relates to my Financial Success Desires looks like…

Being in alignment with _____ (Insert Core Value #3) as it relates to my Financial Success Desires looks like…

What are 3 requests I can make of myself and others to support me in expressing my voice as it relates to my Financial Success desires.

1.

2.

3.

What fears & doubts come up in regards to asking for what you want in these situations?

Core Value #4

Not being in alignment with _____(Insert Core Value #4) as it relates to my Financial Success Desires looks like...

Being in alignment with _____ (Insert Core Value #4) as it relates to my Financial Success Desires looks like…

What are 3 requests I can make of myself and others to support me in expressing my voice as it relates to my Financial Success desires.

1.

2.

3.

What fears & doubts come up in regards to asking for what you want in these situations?

Core Value #5

Not being in alignment with _____(Insert Core Value #5) as it relates to my Financial Success Desires looks like…

Being in alignment with _____ (Insert Core Value #5) as it relates to my Financial Success Desires looks like…

What are 3 requests I can make of myself and others to support me in expressing my voice as it relates to my Financial Success desires.

1.

2.

3.

What fears & doubts come up in regards to asking for what you want in these situations?

Reflections on what it would take for Me to experience Effortless Happiness when it comes to my…

Professional/Career Desires

What would effortless happiness look like as it relates to my Professional/Career Desires?

Core Value #1

Not being in alignment with _____ (Insert Core Value #1) as it relates to my Professional/Career Desires looks like…

Being in alignment with _____ (Insert Core Value #1) as it relates to my Professional/Career Desires looks like…

What are 3 requests I can make of myself and others to support me in expressing my voice as it relates to my Professional/Career desires.

1.

2.

3.

What fears & doubts come up in regards to asking for what you want in these situations?

Core Value #2

Not being in alignment with _____ (Insert Core Value #2) as it relates to my Professional/Career Desires looks like…

Being in alignment with _____ (Insert Core Value #2) as it relates to my Professional/Career Desires looks like…

What are 3 requests I can make of myself and others to support me in expressing my voice as it relates to my Professional/Career desires.

1.

2.

3

What fears & doubts come up in regards to asking for what you want in these situations?

Core Value #3

Not being in alignment with _____(Insert Core Value #3) as it relates to my Professional/Career Desires looks like...

Being in alignment with _____(Insert Core Value #3) as it relates to my Professional/Career Desires looks like…

What are 3 requests I can make of myself and others to support me in expressing my voice as it relates to my Professional/Career desires.

1.

2.

3.

What fears & doubts come up in regards to asking for what you want in these situations?

Core Value #4

Not being in alignment with _____(Insert Core Value #4) as it relates to my Professional/Career Desires looks like…

Being in alignment with _____ (Insert Core Value #4) as it relates to my Professional/Career Desires looks like…

What are 3 requests I can make of myself and others to support me in expressing my voice as it relates to my Professional/Career desires.

1.

2.

3.

What fears & doubts come up in regards to asking for what you want in these situations?

Core Value #5

Not being in alignment with _____(Insert Core Value #5) as it relates to my Professional/Career Desires looks like…

Being in alignment with _____ (Insert Core Value #5) as it relates to my Professional/Career Desires looks like…

What are 3 requests I can make of myself and others to support me in expressing my voice as it relates to my Professional/Career desires.

1.

2.

3.

What fears & doubts come up in regards to asking for what you want in these situations?

Reflections on what it would take for Me to experience Effortless Happiness when it comes to my...

Personal Relationships Desires

What would effortless happiness look like as it relates to my Personal Relationships Desires?

Core Value #1

Not being in alignment with _____ (Insert Core Value #1) as it relates to my Personal Relationships Desires looks like...

Being in alignment with _____ (Insert Core Value #1) as it relates to my Personal Relationships Desires looks like…

What are 3 requests I can make of myself and others to support me in expressing my voice as it relates to my Personal Relationships desires.

1.

2.

3.

What fears & doubts come up in regards to asking for what you want in these situations?

Core Value #2

Not being in alignment with _____(Insert Core Value #2) as it relates to my Personal Relationships Desires looks like…

Being in alignment with _____ (Insert Core Value #2) as it relates to my Personal Relationships Desires looks like…

What are 3 requests I can make of myself and others to support me in expressing my voice as it relates to my Personal Relationships desires.

1.

2.

3.

What fears & doubts come up in regards to asking for what you want in these situations?

Core Value #3

Not being in alignment with _____(Insert Core Value #3) as it relates to my Personal Relationships Desires looks like…

Being in alignment with _____(Insert Core Value #3) as it relates to my Personal Relationships Desires looks like…

What are 3 requests I can make of myself and others to support me in expressing my voice as it relates to my Personal Relationships desires.

1.

2.

3.

What fears & doubts come up in regards to asking for what you want in these situations?

Core Value #4

Not being in alignment with _____(Insert Core Value #4) as it relates to my Personal Relationships Desires looks like…

Being in alignment with _____(Insert Core Value #4) as it relates to my Personal Relationships Desires looks like…

What are 3 requests I can make of myself and others to support me in expressing my voice as it relates to my Personal Relationships desires.

1.

2.

3.

What fears & doubts come up in regards to asking for what you want in these situations?

Core Value #5

Not being in alignment with _____(Insert Core Value #5) as it relates to my Personal Relationships Desires looks like...

Being in alignment with _____ (Insert Core Value #5) as it relates to my Personal Relationships Desires looks like…

What are 3 requests I can make of myself and others to support me in expressing my voice as it relates to my Personal Relationships desires.

1.

2.

3.

What fears & doubts come up in regards to asking for what you want in these situations?

Real happiness is so simple that most people do not recognize it. They think it comes from doing something on a big scale, from a big fortune, or from some great achievement, when, in fact, it is derived from the simplest, the quietest, the most unpretentious things in the world

– Orison S. Marden

Being Conscious of Your Values

You have done a magnificent job of connecting with your core values if you completed the previous exercises.

Your values must become part of you. Without your values being part of your conscious thinking process they remain lifeless abstractions.

You want them to be integral parts of decisions on a course of action. Without this important step, you will find yourself triggered by situations which come into direct conflict with one of your core values:

Let me share a personal story as an example of a real life reality check.

It was my daughter's wedding at a remote beach resort. The resort had promised my daughter a private beach for her special day.

The dress rehearsal the night before had come off beautifully. Everything was perfect and we were all anticipating a wonderful ceremony.

The night of the wedding, the "private" beach was a sea of guests in bathing suits, drinking beer, and really enjoying themselves just 20 feet away from my only daughter's wedding location.

As the mother of the bride, and wanting my daughter's wedding to go as she had envisioned, I immediately became angry with the hotel management.

When I saw the confusion, I tried to change the situation. Then I realized the confusion and contrast was in my thoughts and values compared to my daughter's values. Her focus was on her wedding vows and not values at that moment.

FLASH: One of my core values is HONESTY. I felt the hotel had violated that value by not providing the private beach.

FLASH: My daughter's top core values were not "honesty" and so she was not affected by the honesty issue. On the contrary, she was filled with happiness!

She wasn't bothered at all by the uninvited guests attending her wedding. She could only see her new husband waiting for her as she walked to the beach.

SOLUTION: I had a choice to accept or not accept my daughter's value and enjoy the beauty of her special day in this special place.

Once I took my expectations off of me and allowed her values to take precedent, I could calm myself and enjoy the wedding.

It was a gorgeous wedding! But it challenged me to be consciously aware of my values vs. the values of my daughter.

Your values guide and influence your expectations and decisions. But, now that you are conscious of them you can be much more intentional about how you direct your decisions and situations where they can cause conflict with others.

Remember, life is a journey. Wisely we will continue to self-correct as we know ourselves better.

I've come to believe that each of us has a personal calling that's as unique as a fingerprint - and that the best way to succeed is to discover what you love and then find a way to offer it to others in the form of service, working hard, and also allowing the energy of the universe to lead you.

— Oprah Winfrey

Conclusion

You have now completed the Core Values elimination exercise and identified the values that are most important to you. Now you will want to use these values in your life.

Print off the core values certificate (instructions are on the next page) and put it up where you will see it every day.

Tell your friends and family about the core values that "matter the most to you" and ask them how they see it demonstrated in your life.

With time and change of life you will want to use the workbook to go through this exercise again. Core values can change in relationships as to the importance in your life.

Example:

When raising younger children, your children are probably in your top 5 Core Values. As they become adult children these values may be lower in your priorities.

I hope that you have found this process encouraging and enlightening. Use your newfound focus and clarity to live an authentic life. Pursue the happiness and peace that comes with allowing your core values to guide you.

No matter what life has handed you, you can use your core values to guide your pursuit of the life you were meant to live, a life of effortless happiness!

Please Visit

http://JoyceBufordEmpowers.com/Core-Values-Certificate

to print out your Core Values Certificate.

Every single moment that you are faced with a decision to make, take a look at your core values certificate to see if you are in alignment.

CORE VALUES AWARD

PRESENTED TO:

WHOSE CORE VALUES ARE:

Joyce Buford
Joyce Buford,
Creator of the Uncover Your Hidden Genius Program

"Let your values guide you to effortless happiness"

-Joyce Buford

Effortless Happiness Strategy Session

Yes, Joyce, I'm Ready to Uncover My Hidden Genius and Discover How to Live My Life in Alignment with my Core Values. I'm Ready for My Customized **'Effortless Happiness'** Strategy Session!

During our time together I understand I'll walk away with the following benefits:

- Create clarity around the life you really want to live.
- Find out the essential building blocks for having a life filled with effortless happiness.
- Discover the #1 thing stopping you from living your passions and purpose.
- Identify the most powerful actions that will move you forward towards happiness.
- Complete the consultation with the excitement of knowing EXACTLY what to do next to create a life of effortless happiness.

To schedule your complimentary Effortless Happiness Strategy Session Visit
http://JoyceBufordEmpowers/Effortless-Happiness/

SecondWind Podcast

I hope you've enjoyed working through your core values. I love to see people reconnect with their natural talents and passions. That's why I love talking with men and women who have successfully transitioned from stressful and struggling lives into new careers and fresh starts.

My *SecondWind* Podcast is a program focused for and about women and men who need a fresh start. *SecondWind* focuses on days of successful transitions. Examples of life transitions are "empty nest", new job or retirement, divorce or death of a loved one, as well as parent life transitions, to name a few. Each week I speak with a different authority discussing these and other topics. If you tune in, I promise you will walk away with tools for transitioning smoothly as well as valuable recourses offered by my guests.

You can find my *SecondWind* Podcast on ITunes.

One of my favorite podcasts is:

Tools for Managing your Stress with Dr. Richard Blonna

Dr. Rich has devoted the past 25 years to helping individuals create and manage stress. He is a noted writer and trainer and he is also certified in Naikan and Morita which are two forms of Japanese psychology that emphasize mindfulness and acceptance training respectively.

In this podcast we discuss several topics, such as, the different types of stress, and how our bodies are affected by them. As well as how living your life not in alignment with your Core Values can cause an increase of stress in your life.

Find it here:

http://joycebufordempowers.com/stress-less-live/

One of my favorite podcasts is:

What is Intentional Possibility with Dr. Sergio Sedas

Dr. Sedas is a bestselling author and is recognized internationally as a high-potential trainer. He implements intentional possibility to bring about positive transformation in life, communities, and organizations. Through it all he has maintained a passion for education and was led to one of the leading Technological Universities in Monterrey, Mexico.

On this segment of *SecondWind* we discuss what intentional possibility is, as well as how we all possess the Power of Possibility and the six steps to creating possibility.

Find it here:

http://joycebufordempowers.com/what-is-intentional-possibility

One of my favorite podcasts is:

How does Transition Shape your Career with Michele Moore

Michele Moore is a consultant to educational institutions, nonprofits, and entrepreneurs. She helps them to implement new programs and initiatives.

Her lifelong interests focus on the actions between humans and animals, and implementing the integration of animals into the health care system.

She shares her journey as she transitioned from 12 years in administration and as an effective leader in higher education to owning her own business.

She is now working and living with passion.

Find it here:

http://joycebufordempowers.com/great-day

One of my favorite podcasts is:

Make More Money with Marie Fratoni

QUEEN of connecting, Marie Fratoni, is the CEO of *Get Clients Everywhere*. She helps professionals build solid, long-term, successful businesses on a global scale and coaches them to become savvy, social, and successful through cultivating professional relationships that are both fulfilling and profitable.

Marie discusses how transitions affect women's business attitudes. Many professional women want to create something of their own that is more aligned with their passion, talent and desire to make a difference. Marie provides insight on what guidelines women should follow whenever they begin to move forward and branch out on their own.

Find it here:

http://joycebufordempowers.com/make-more-money

One of my favorite podcasts is:

Remove the Clutter from your Life with Marcella Scherer

Marcella Scherer, sought after speaker, bestselling author, and founder of her own image consulting business.

Marcella discusses using her knowledge to empower women to unveil their true and authentic selves and command the attention they deserve.

She also discusses some helpful tips for removing clutter from various areas of your life as well as how that can further your transformation into the woman that you want to be!

Find it here:

http://joycebufordempowers.com/remove-clutter-life

One of my favorite podcasts is:

Rodan and Fields Believes Skincare is Serious Business

Gillian Sheridan and Stacey Hiles, Consultants with *Rodan and Fields,* reveal the benefits of these life changing Skin Care Products. Rodan and Fields states it's universal quest is for perfect skin. Known as the prescription for change, Rodan and Fields are two women dermatologists who took the problems of skin care through 4 systems addressing acne, wrinkles, aging, and sensitivity.

They heard a compelling message from their mentor, the director of the Dermatology Department: Find your purpose and make a difference or be confined to a career that's ordinary: Go forth and change the rules.

And so they did.

Find it here:

http://joycebufordempowers.com/skincare

One of my favorite podcasts is:

How can Soulful Intuition help your business?

Kathy Knowles has been recognized by the Southern Florida Business Journal as a human resource leader, and is the creator of the program *Why Your Business is Stealing Your Soul - 7 Steps for Creating more Pleasure, Profits, and Possibilities.* Kathy helps guide women entrepreneurs to achieve a greater life with greater happiness. Kathy has 20 years of experience working with an award winning multi-million-dollar company.

She discusses the definition of "Soul" and the necessity of knowing how your soul is guiding you.

Find it here:

http://joycebufordempowers.com/soulful-intuition

One of my favorite podcasts is:

Journal through Transition with Janet Wiszowaty

Janet Wiszowaty, a Visionary, Consultant, and Founder of Family Connekt, shares the importance of understanding that life is a choice.

As a First Response Emergency Dispatcher, Janet was experiencing Post Traumatic Stress Disorder. In her healing, Janet found the importance of using positive tools and positive people to help her overcome obstacles and transitions in her life.

One of the tools Janet used quite successfully was Journaling. Today she helps other clients transition by using journaling in their lives to move through grief and pain.

Find it here:

http://joycebufordempowers.com/journal-through-transition

One of my favorite podcasts is:

Rock Your Mojo through Midlife with Dr. Anna Garrett

Dr. Anna Garrett, Menopause Expert, Women's Health Educator and Advocate, and Chief Mojo Officertalks about how aging affects not only our bodies but our minds as well.

Anna discuss the differences between menopause and perimenopause. Understanding how you can stop the symptoms from taking over your life is necessary to mid-life enjoyment.

Listen in and learn how to continue to rock your mojo through midlife!

Find it here:

http://joycebufordempowers.com/rock-your-mojo

Are You Ready to Uncover Your Hidden Genius?

As we discussed previously identifying your core values is just the first step in Uncovering Your Hidden Genius program. This program will take you from living a life of hardship and frustration to a life of ease, happiness and financial freedom.

During this program you will:

- Know and be able to implement your vision for 7 areas of your life: Health and Fitness, Spiritual, Contribution, Personal, Financial, Professional, Relationships/ Family and Friends.
- Develop goals based on Core Values and Your visions – not just meaningless someday to-do list.
- Identify your uniqueness
- Find your purpose
- Map out a strategy for creating success
- and much more!

If you are interested in finding out if this program is a fit for you, please schedule a time to talk with Joyce at:

http://JoyceBufordEmpowers.com/Uncover-Your-Hidden-Genius/

www.ingramcontent.com/pod-product-compliance
Lightning Source LLC
Chambersburg PA
CBHW051126160426
43195CB00014B/2357